D1367072

People of the Bible

The Bible through stories and pictures

Noah and His Ark

Copyright © in this format Belitha Press Ltd, 1982

Illustrations copyright © Jim Russell 1982

Art Director: Treld Bicknell

First published in the United States of America 1982
by Raintree Publishers, Inc.
205 West Highland Avenue, Milwaukee, Wisconsin 53203
in association with Belitha Press Ltd, London.

Conceived, designed and produced by Belitha Press Ltd,
40 Belitha Villas, London N1 1PD

Moody Press Edition 1983
ISBN: 0-8024-0396-4

First published in Australia in paperback 1982
by Princeton Books Pty Ltd, PO Box 24, Cheltenham, Victoria 3192
in association with Raintree Childrens Books
205 West Highland Avenue, Milwaukee, Wisconsin 53203

ISBN 0 909091 19 6 (Australian)

Printed in Hong Kong
by South China Printing Co.

Noah and His Ark

RETOLD BY ELLA K. LINDVALL
PICTURES BY JIM RUSSELL

MOODY PRESS
CHICAGO

Once upon a time there lived a man called Noah. He had a wife and three sons—Shem, Ham, and Japheth. The sons had wives, too.

Noah's family loved God and tried to please Him. But the rest of the people in the world tried to please just themselves.

Now when people forget God and think only about pleasing themselves, bad things are sure to happen. Everybody except Noah's family grew worse and worse. People hated each other and hurt each other.

God saw what was happening, and He was sad.

One day, Noah heard God say to him,
"Noah! There is going to be a great flood, and
the wicked people will be drowned. Only you
and your family will be left alive.

"You must start at once to build a huge ship, with a window and a door and rooms. It must be big enough to hold you and your family and two of every kind of animal."

Noah started to obey. First, he called his three sons, Shem, Ham, and Japheth. They went up the mountainside and cut down trees and sawed them into boards. They began to build the huge ship. They called it the Ark.

Noah's neighbors must have come out and laughed at him. "What a stupid thing to do!" they said. "Why build a ship like this, miles away from the sea?"

"Because God told me to," Noah answered. "He is going to send a great flood of water on the earth."

But that only made them laugh more.

At last the Ark was finished. Then the animals began to come—bears, zebras, cats, rabbits, mice, even spiders and ants. God sent them.

Two of every kind came into the Ark and were put into the stables, the cages, and the rooms where they were to live.

Then, when the last animal was safe inside, and Noah and his family were safe inside, God shut the door.

At first, Noah's neighbors probably went on laughing. They said, "What in the world will Noah do in there with all those animals?"

But soon great black clouds came. The sky grew dark. And the first raindrops began to fall.

Down came water from the sky. Up came water from the ground. First it covered the roads and the fields. Then it came up to the windows of the houses. Then it came up to the roofs of the houses and the tops of the trees.

At last there was nothing to be seen in the whole world except the Ark, floating all alone in a world of water. Still it went on raining.

But inside the Ark everyone was safe and dry.

Noah told his family what to do. Maybe he said, "Shem, you and your wife must feed all the animals. We have plenty of leaves and corn for the elephants and the rabbits. The cow will give you milk for the cats. Don't let them eat the mice.

"Ham," Noah might have said, "you and your wife must keep the animals clean. Sweep out the stables and wash the cages."

Maybe he told Japheth, "You and your wife must collect the rain water as it falls on the Ark, so that we will have fresh water to drink and to wash with.

"Your mother is going to cook for all of us,
and I will help everybody."

After forty long days and nights, at last the rain stopped. There was no dry land to be seen anywhere.

Slowly, slowly the water went down, until one day—bump!—the Ark came to rest on the top of a high mountain. Later, Noah could see other mountaintops.

Noah waited. Then he sent out a raven to look for land. The big black bird flew and flew and did not come back. Then Noah sent out a dove. But the dove could not find any land, and she flew back to the Ark to rest.

A week later, Noah sent out the dove again. That evening she came back with a leaf from an olive tree in her beak. Then Noah knew that soon they would see dry land again.

After another seven days, Noah sent out the dove once more. This time she did not come back at all. He knew she had found a dry place where she could build her nest.

Noah still waited for God to tell him what to do. At last he heard God say, "Go out of the Ark now—you and your family and the animals—and live on the earth again."

All the animals were very glad to get out. Noah said to them, "Go off, stretch your legs, eat all you can find, and have lots of babies to fill this empty world."

Noah and his family were glad to get out of the Ark, too. The first thing they did was to thank God for taking care of them.

At first they wondered if someday there might be another flood over all the world, but God promised that would never happen again.

To show that He would remember His promise, God put a rainbow in the sky.

So Noah and his family began to build houses and plant gardens again. They knew God would do what He promised. He always does.

Moody Press, a ministry of the Moody Bible Institute, is designed for education, evangelization, and edification. If we may assist you in knowing more about Christ and the Christian life, please write us without obligation: Moody Press, c/o MLM, Chicago, Illinois 60610.

The Land of the Bible Today

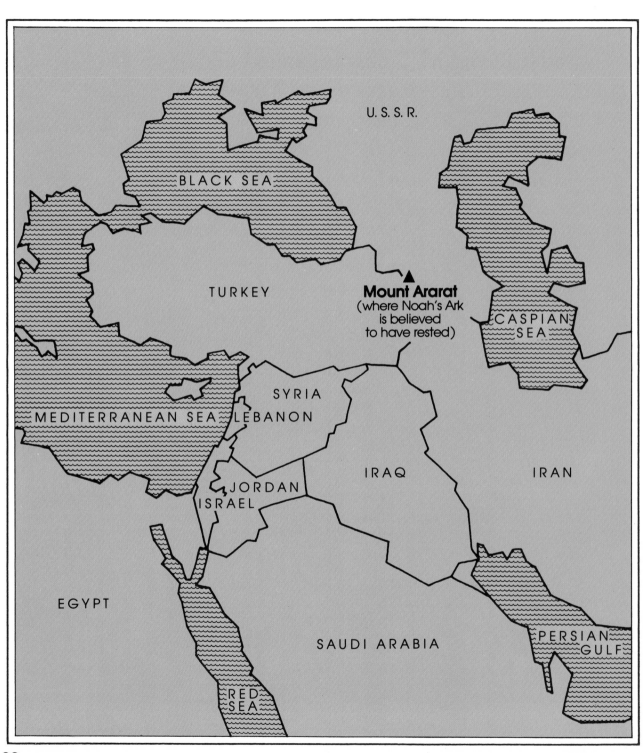

U. S. S. R.

BLACK SEA

TURKEY

Mount Ararat
(where Noah's Ark
is believed
to have rested)

CASPIAN
SEA

SYRIA
LEBANON

MEDITERRANEAN SEA

IRAQ

IRAN

JORDAN
ISRAEL

EGYPT

SAUDI ARABIA

PERSIAN
GULF

RED
SEA